How to **Knit** Fashionable
scarves
on **Circle Looms**™

Designs by Denise Layman

HOUSE of
WHITE
BIRCHES

PUBLISHERS
SINCE 1947

Introduction

If you've tried your hand at circle looms, or would like to learn how, *How to Knit Fashionable Scarves on Circle Looms* will take your skills to a new level and show you how easy knitting on circle looms can be! Learn new stitches and techniques to create a variety of great scarves for everyone you know and love. The 12 patterns within will expand your loom-knitting know-how.

This book will show you how to use your circle looms in ways you thought only possible on knitting needles. Create lightweight lace with the Westminster Eyelet Scarf or add a side of fringe with the Trafalgar Self-Fringing Scarf. Maybe you'd like to put your loom to the test with the Bloomsbury Chain-Link Scarf. And if you're so inclined, you can even learn how to add beaded embellishments with the Hampstead Beaded Scarf.

With so many new options to explore, *How to Knit Fashionable Scarves on Circle Looms* will empower you to take your experience as a loom knitter to new and inspiring places!

Table of Contents

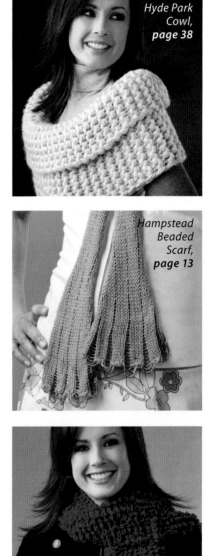

Hyde Park Cowl, page 38

Hampstead Beaded Scarf, page 13

Piccadilly Scarf, page 22

Oxford Mitered Scarf, page 10

Soho Neck Warmer, page 34

Camden Scarf, page 32

General Directions

The patterns in this book were all made and written as if the loom was being worked in a clockwise direction, so all patterns start at the starting peg on the loom and are worked to the left as the loom is held facing you. However, any pattern in this book can be worked in the counterclockwise direction by simply following the patterns as written.

Materials

Knifty Knitter looms from Provo Craft*

Loom tool

Crochet hook

Yarn or tapestry needle

Photographed items were designed using Knifty Knitter circle looms; other circular looms may be used, but the gauge may differ slightly.

Casting On

Purl Cast-On Method

1. E-wrap to one less than the desired number of stitches.

2. Bring the working yarn between the last wrapped peg and the next empty peg to the front of the loom, and then around the far edge of the next peg into the center of the loom (Photo 1).

3. Bring the working yarn back between the two pegs to the front of the loom so that the working yarn is in position to be purled on the first e-wrapped peg on the return row (Photo 2).

4. Purl on the return row.

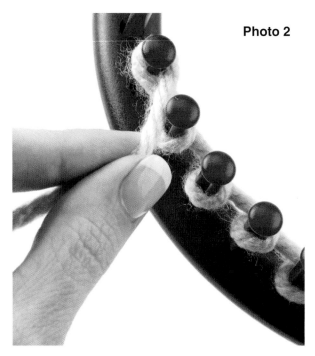

Photo 2

Photo 1

E-wrap Cast-On Method

1. Make a slip knot about 6 inches from the end of the yarn. Place it on peg 1.

2. Starting from the inside of the loom, bring the working yarn between pegs 2 and 3 to the outside of the loom. Continue wrapping peg 2, bringing the working yarn between pegs 2 and 1 to the inside of the loom.

3. The yarn will cross over itself on the inside of peg 2 as it travels to peg 3.

4. Continue wrapping the pegs until the desired number of pegs have loops on them (Photo 3).

Photo 3

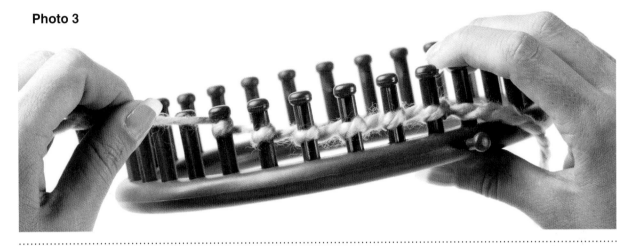

Basic Stitches

Knit Stitch

1. To make a knit stitch without a twist, bring the working yarn to the front of the loom above the previous stitch on the peg (Photo 4).

2. Bring the yarn slightly behind the peg, forming a little hook around the peg, and pull the lower stitch over the working yarn and off the peg (Photos 5 and 6).

3. Move working yarn to next peg and repeat.

Photo 4

Photo 5

Photo 6

Purl Stitch

1. Wrap one loop on number of pegs as directed in the pattern.

2. Lay your working yarn across the front of the pegs, just below the first wrapped loop (Photo 7).

Photo 7

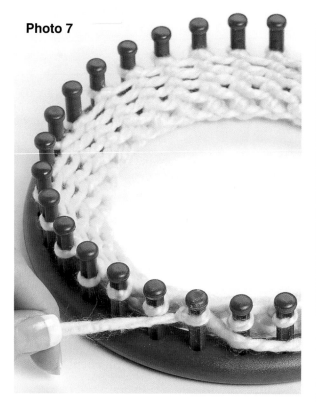

3. Using your knitting tool, reach down through the wrapped loop on the first peg and pull the working yarn up through the loop, forming another loop (Photo 8).

Photo 8

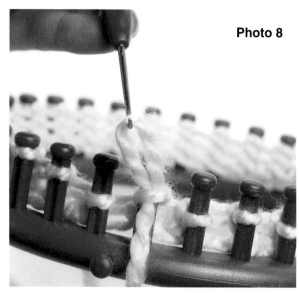

4. Pull the original wrapped loop off the peg, and place the newly formed loop on the peg. Tug gently on the working yarn to secure the loop on the peg (Photo 9).

Photo 9

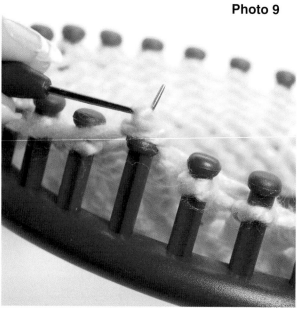

5. Move to the next peg and repeat stitch as called for in the pattern.

Garter Stitch

Garter stitch is the knit pattern created by knitting one row, and then purling the next row.

Knit 2 Together (k2tog)

1. Move the loop from one peg onto the adjacent peg.

2. Knit both loops over the working yarn to knit the two together.

Yarn Over (yo)

Run the working yarn in front of the empty peg left by a k2tog or a space left by moving stitches away from each other to increase. On the next row, this strand will be knit or purled according to the pattern.

Bind Off

Gather Bind-Off Method

1. Once the piece reaches the desired length, wrap your working yarn around the loom one and a half times; cut the yarn.

2. Using a yarn needle, thread the working yarn through each loop on the loom. Start with the loop to the left of the holding peg and work in a clockwise direction all the way around the loom (Photo 10).

3. Thread the working yarn through the loop to the left of the holding peg a second time.

4. Remove the loops from the loom and gently tug on the yarn tail until the piece gathers tightly together. Using the needle, secure the working yarn on the inside of the piece (Photo 11).

5. Turn the piece inside out and weave in the ends.

Photo 10

Photo 11

Flat-Piece Bind-Off Method

1. Work piece until desired length as directed in pattern.

2. Turn and slip the first stitch as if to start another row (Photo 12).

3. Knit or purl the next stitch in the row as per pattern.

4. Take the stitch loop just formed and place it on the peg with the previous stitch (Photo 13).

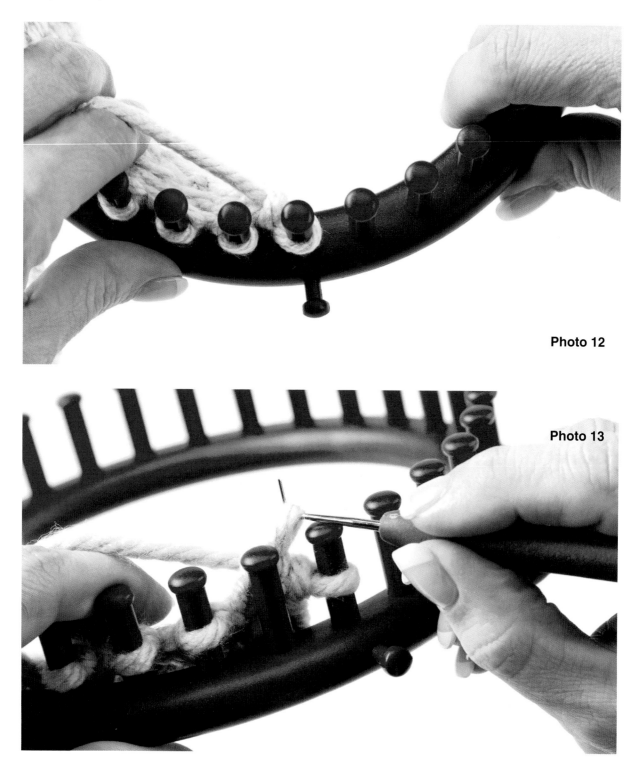

Photo 12

Photo 13

5. Knit the stitch over.

6. Place the stitch back on the peg from which it was moved (Photos 14 and 15).

7. Move to the next stitch in the row and repeat from step 3.

8. Continue in this manner across the row. ●

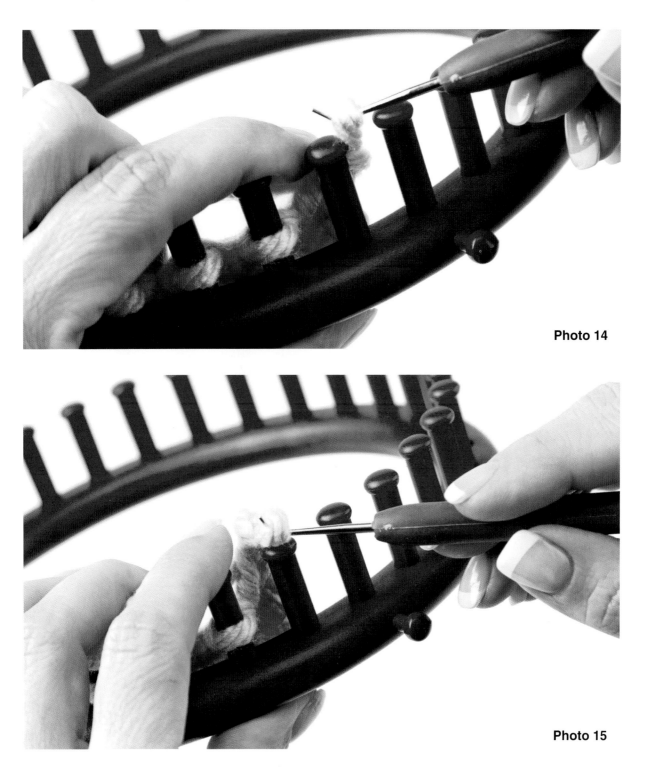

Photo 14

Photo 15

Oxford Mitered Scarf

Mitered squares are a great way to show off self-striping yarns. The technique is simple and yields beautiful results.

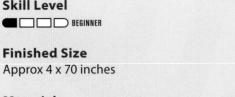

Skill Level
◖◻◻◻ BEGINNER

Finished Size
Approx 4 x 70 inches

Materials
- Patons Classic Wool (worsted weight; 100% wool; 210 yds/100g per skein): 2 skeins harvest #77236
- Red Knifty Knitter circle loom (31 pegs)
- Stitch marker
- Large-eye yarn needle
- Loom tool

4 MEDIUM

Gauge
4 inches = 13 sts, 18 rows in garter st pat.

Exact gauge is not critical to this project.

Special Abbreviation
Knit 3 together (k3tog): As shown in Photos 1–5, move the loops on the pegs on either side of the center peg onto the center peg, so that there are 3 loops on this peg. *Note: For uniformity, be sure to move the sts in the same order each time. Move the other sts in toward the center st as needed, so that there are no longer any empty pegs.*

Photo 2

Photo 3

Photo 4

Photo 1

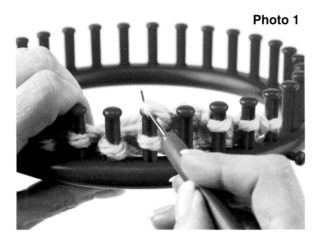

Photo 5

Special Technique

Making mitered squares: To make a basic mitered square, start with an odd amount of sts. Mark the center st with a st marker.

Cast on, turn and purl 1 row.

On the next row, which will be a knit row, make a double dec using k3tog.

On the next row, purl.

Be sure to always move the loops in the same order so that the double dec has a consistent look throughout.

Instructions

E-wrap cast on (see page 5) 31 pegs, turn and purl the first row.

Beg mitered square pat:

Row 1: K14, k3tog, k14.

Row 2: Purl.

Row 3: K13, k3tog, k13.

Row 4: Purl.

Row 5: K12, k3tog, k12.

Rows 6–22: Rep Rows 1–5 consecutively, knitting 1 less st on each end of odd-numbered rows, ending with a purl row. *(11 sts—5 on each end and 1 in center)*

Row 23: Knit all sts, wrapping 10 pegs at end of row.

Row 24: Purl all sts, wrapping 10 pegs at end of row.

Rows 25–48: Rep Rows 1–24 of mitered square pat.

Rep Rows 1–24 of mitered square pat for a total of 15 squares or until scarf is 1 square from desired length.

Final Square

Rep Rows 1–22 until only 1 st rem on the loom.

Fasten off and pull end of yarn through rem st to secure and remove scarf from the loom.

Finishing

Block scarf as desired and weave in ends. ●

Hampstead Beaded Scarf

The drops of beads add sparkle and help create the shaping of this great beginner scarf.

Skill Level

◼◻◻◻ BEGINNER

Finished Size
Approx 4 x 60 inches

Materials
- NaturallyCaron.com Spa (light weight; 75% micro-denier acrylic/25% rayon from bamboo; 251 yds/85g per skein): 2 skeins green sheen #0004
- Green Knifty Knitter circle loom (36 pegs)
- Large-eye yarn needle
- Loom tool
- G-6 (4mm) crochet hook
- #6 seed beads: approx 640 green
- Bead threader

Gauge
4 inches = 22 sts, 18 rows in garter st pat.

Exact gauge is not critical to this project.

Pattern Notes
Scarf is made in 2 halves, starting with the beaded cast on. Scarf is joined at the center of the back of the neck.

The letter "B" followed by a number in the pattern refers to the number of beads to be slid snugly against a peg before knitting the next stitches.

Instructions
Make 2

String approx 320 beads onto yarn using a bead threader. As you work, unwind a small quantity of yarn, each time sliding the beads toward the ball until needed. Pass the yarn through the loop of the threader and pick up beads with the working end of the needle (see Knitting With Beads, page 44).

Slide the beads over the loop and onto the yarn. Referring to illustrations below, make a slip knot in your yarn, place on a crochet hook and ch 2.

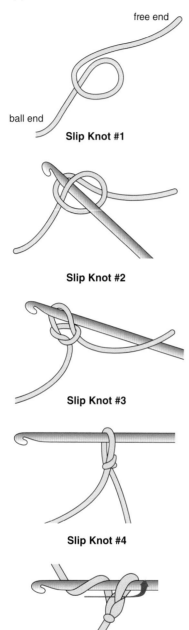

Slip Knot #1

Slip Knot #2

Slip Knot #3

Slip Knot #4

Chain Stitch

Place slip knot and 2 chained stitches onto the first 3 pegs of the loom.

Slide up 6 beads snug against peg 3.

*Create a slip knot snug up against the beads and ch 3 with crochet hook.

Place slip knot and 3 chained stitches on next 4 pegs of the loom.

Slide up 6 beads.

Rep from * 2 times.

Create a slip knot snug up against the beads and ch 2 with crochet hook.

Place slip knot and 2 chained stitches on next 3 empty pegs on the loom.

Pattern

Row 1: K3, B6, k4, B6, k4, B6, k4, B6, k4, B6, k3.

Row 2: K3, B5, k4, B5, k4, B5, k4, B5, k4, B5, k3.

Row 3: K3, B5, k4 , B5, k4, B5, k4, B5, k4, B5, k3.

Row 4: K3, B4, k4, B4, k4, B4, k4, B4, k4, B4, k3.

Row 5: K3, B4, k4 , B4, k4, B4, k4, B4, k4, B4, k3.

Row 6: K3, B3, k4, B3, k4, B3, k4, B3, k4, B3, k3.

Row 7: K3, B3, k4, B3, k4, B3, k4, B3, k4, B3, k3.

Row 8: K3, B2, k4, B2, k4, B3, k4, B2, k4, B2, k3.

Row 9: K3, B2, k4, B2, k4, B2, k4, B2, k4, B2, k3.

Row 10: K3, B1, k4, B1, k4, B2, k4, B1, k4, B1, k3.

Row 11: K3, B1, k4, B1, k4, B1, k4, B1, k4, B1, k3.

Rows 12–18: [Rep Row 11] 7 times.

Row 19: K7, B1, k4, B1, k4, B1, k7.

Row 20: K3, B1, k4, B1, k4, B1, k4, B1, k4, B1, k3.

Rows 21–26: [Rep Rows 19 and 20] 3 times.

Row 27: K7, B1, k4, B1, k4, B1, k7.

Row 28: Knit.

Row 29: K3, B1, k4, B1, k4, B1, k4, B1, k4, B1, k3.

Row 30: K7, B1, k4, B1, k4, B1, k7.

Rows 31–38: [Rep Rows 24–27] twice.

Row 39: Knit.

Row 40: K11, B1, k11.

Next rows: [Rep Rows 39 and 40] until all beads are used.

Continue to knit each row until scarf is half of the desired length.

Bind off using flat-piece bind-off method (see page 8).

Finishing
Join 2 halves tog at unbeaded ends. Block scarf as desired. ●

Notting Hill Tube Scarf

If you have an affinity for funky, chunky designs, this scarf captures that big, bold look of the 1980s.

Skill Level
◼☐☐☐ BEGINNER

Finished Size
Approx 5 x 70 inches

Materials
- Stitch Nation Full o' Sheep (worsted weight; 100% wool; 155 yds/100g per skein): 4 skeins plummy #2550
- Red Knifty Knitter circle loom (31 pegs)
- Stitch marker
- Large-eye yarn needle
- Loom tool
- 9½-inch square cardboard

4 MEDIUM

Gauge
4 inches = 13 sts, 18 rows in garter st pat.

Exact gauge is not critical to this project.

Instructions
Leaving a 12-inch tail, e-wrap cast on (see page 5) entire loom.

Row 1: Knit.

Rep Row 1, working in the rnd, until scarf is desired length.

Bind off using the gather bind-off method (see page 7).

Finishing
Make 2 large tassels
Wrap yarn around cardboard 100 times. Tie length of yarn tightly around the middle of the strands at top of cardboard. Remove yarn from cardboard and cut through loops at bottom of tassel. Wrap another length of yarn several times around yarn about 2 inches down from top of tassel. Tie off yarn and tuck in ends. Trim any uneven pieces of yarn. ●

Bloomsbury Chain-Link Scarf

This simple scarf is easier than you think—each link is finished and joined to the scarf as it comes off the loom. No seaming required!

Skill Level
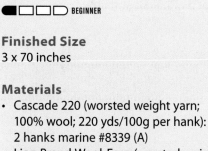
◖☐☐☐ BEGINNER

Finished Size
3 x 70 inches

Materials
- Cascade 220 (worsted weight yarn; 100% wool; 220 yds/100g per hank): 2 hanks marine #8339 (A)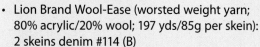
- Lion Brand Wool-Ease (worsted weight yarn; 80% acrylic/20% wool; 197 yds/85g per skein): 2 skeins denim #114 (B)
- Blue Knifty Knitter circle loom (24 pegs)
- Stitch marker
- Large-eye yarn needle
- Loom tool

Gauge
4 inches = 16 sts, 18 rows in garter st pat.

Exact gauge is not critical to this project.

Instructions

First Link
With A, e-wrap cast on (see page 5) 12 pegs.

Row 1: Purl.

Row 2: Knit.

Row 3: Purl.

Rows 4–125: Rep Rows 2 and 3 alternately, ending with a knit row.

Bring the loops from the cast-on edge up and place onto the corresponding pegs of the loom.

Bind off by purling the 2 loops tog and then casting off each st in the row.

Turn link loop inside out so that the cast-off joint ridge is on the inside of the link loop.

Second Link
With B, rep Rows 1–125 of first link.

Pull the cast-on end of the working link up through the center of the first link and place onto the corresponding pegs of the loom.

Bind off by purling the 2 loops tog and then casting off each st in the row.

Remaining Links
Continue in this manner, making link loops and attaching them to the previous link just prior to casting off each link loop.

Work each link loop, alternating colors A and B or in color pat desired.

Work until scarf has reached desired length.

Finishing
Make sure to turn each link inside out so that the cast-off ridge is on the inside of the link.

To help hide these ridge bumps, using the 6-inch tail left at the end of each link and holding the cast-off ridge edges of 2 links tog, join where the cast-off ridges meet.

Continue to join the cast-off end of the links tog until all are joined in this manner.

Weave in any loose ends. •

Trafalgar Self-Fringing Scarf

This whimsical scarf adds fringe as you go, creating style and flair with no fussy finishing!

Skill Level
■□□□ BEGINNER

Finished Size
Approx 4 x 70 inches

Materials
- Premier Mega Brushed (worsted weight; 100% acrylic; 191 yds/3½ oz per skein): 3 skeins Arizona #51-219
- Green Knifty Knitter circle loom (36 pegs)
- Stitch marker
- Large-eye yarn needle
- Loom tool

Gauge
4 inches = 10 sts, 18 rows in garter stitch pat.

Exact gauge is not critical to this project.

Instructions
Purl cast on (see page 4) 12 pegs.

Trail the working yarn along the front of the next 10 pegs and around peg 22 to the inside of the loom. Bring working yarn back to the front of the loom between pegs 13 and 12.

Pattern Stitch

Row 1: K12 sts, bring working yarn to the front of the loom and wrap around the next 10 pegs, bringing the working yarn around peg 22 to the inside of the loom. Bring working yarn back to front of the loom between pegs 13 and 12.

Row 2: Purl all sts. Drop the large fringe loop off the loom into the center of the loom, tug on the loop to set in sts.

Rep Rows 1 and 2 alternately until scarf measures 66 inches or to desired length.

Note: As the scarf is worked, it is best to secure the fringe loops with an overhand knot at the edge of each row. ●

Piccadilly Scarf

This retro-inspired shag-rug scarf is fun to knit and fun to wear!

Photo 3

Do not remove the st from the peg. Bring the working yarn back around the peg in an e-wrap.

Knit the lower st over the e-wrap and flip the loop over the peg to the inside of the loom.

Skill Level
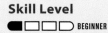 BEGINNER

Finished Size
Approx 6 x 50 inches

Materials
- Cascade 220 Wool (worsted weight; 100% Peruvian Highland wool; 220 yds/100g per hank): 3 hanks dark rose #7802
- Green Knifty Knitter circle loom (36 pegs)
- Stitch marker
- Large-eye yarn needle
- Loom tool

4 MEDIUM

Gauge
Exact gauge is not critical to this project.

Special Technique

Loop stitch (loop st): As shown in photos 1–3, work the st as if to purl, pulling the working yarn up through the loop on the peg and place it on your free thumb in front of the peg to form a larger loop.

Photo 1

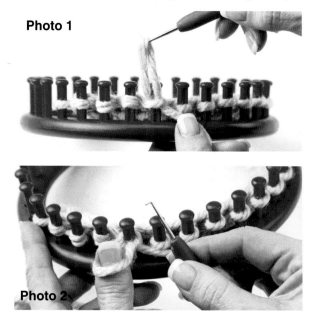

Photo 2

Pattern Notes
Scarf is made with 2 strands of yarn held together as 1 throughout.

It is best to hand wash this scarf as machine washing can pull the loops, making them uneven.

Instructions
Purl cast on (see page 4) 14 pegs.

Row 1: Knit.

Row 2: Purl.

Rows 3–6: [Rep Rows 1 and 2 alternately] twice.

Row 7: Knit.

Row 8: Sl 1, loop st to last st, p1.

Row 9: Sl 1, knit to last st in row, p1.

[Rep Rows 8 and 9 alternately] until scarf measures 48 inches or to desired length.

[Rep Rows 1 and 2] 4 times.

Bind off using flat-piece bind-off method (see page 8).

Finishing
Fold over garter st ends and secure them to the back of scarf. Weave in loose ends and block scarf as desired. ●

Chelsea Hooded Scarf

Make her happy with a hood and built-in fingerless mitts—the main ingredients that make up the core of any wardrobe.

Skill Level
■□□□ BEGINNER

Finished Sizes
Scarf/mitts: Approx 4 x 70 inches
Hood: Approx 9 x 22 inches

Materials
- Lion Brand Alpine Wool (bulky weight; 100% pure wool; 93 yds/85g per skein): 6 skeins bay leaf #123
- Blue Knifty Knitter circle loom (24 pegs) and Yellow Knifty Knitter circle loom (41 pegs)
- Large-eye yarn needle
- Loom tool
- Stitch markers or safety pins

Gauge
4 inches = 16 sts, 18 rows in St st.

Exact gauge is not critical to this project.

Special Abbreviations
Knit 2 together (k2tog): Move the loop from 1 peg onto the adjacent peg. Knit both loops over the working yarn to knit the 2 tog.

Make 1 (M1): Move the st over to next empty peg and e-wrap the empty peg on the next rnd.

Purl 2 together (p2tog): Move the loop from 1 peg onto the adjacent peg. Purl both loops over the working yarn to purl the 2 tog.

Instructions

First Mitt
Using smaller loom, e-wrap cast on (see page 5) 24 pegs.

Rnds 1–10: Working in the rnd, [k2, p2] around entire loom.

Rnd 11 (thumbhole rnd): K2, p1, p2tog, yo, yo, k2tog, k2, p2, work in established rib pat for remainder of rnd.

Rnds 12–31: [K2, p2] around entire loom.

Divide for Scarf
Row 1: K1, k2tog, knit to last 3 sts of row, k2tog, k1.

Row 2: Knit.

[Rep Rows 1 and 2 alternately] until 16 sts rem.

Scarf Body
Row 1: P3, knit to last 3 sts, p3.

Row 2: Knit.

[Rep Rows 1 and 2 alternately] until scarf measures 55 inches long or to desired length.

Inc for 2nd mitt as follows:

Row 1: K1, M1, knit to last st, M1, k1.

Row 2: Knit.

[Rep Rows 1 and 2 alternately] until all pegs on the loom have loops on them, then beg working in the rnd.

Second Mitt
Rnds 1–20: [K2, p2] around entire loom.

Thumbhole Round
Rnd 21: K2, p1, p2tog, yo, yo, k2tog, then work in established rib pat for remainder of rnd.

Rnds 22-31: [K2, p2] around entire loom.

Bind off all pegs in k2, p2 pat using the flat-piece bind-off method (see page 8).

Hood

Using larger loom, e-wrap cast on 40 pegs.

Row 1: Knit.

Rep Row 1 until piece measures 5 inches in length.

Row 2: [K2, p2] across entire row.

Rep Row 2 until piece measures 7 inches in length.

Bind off in pat, using the flat-piece bind-off method.

Finishing

Block the separate pieces of scarf as desired.

Fold the hood piece in half with right sides and ribbed edges together.

Using the mattress stitch, seam the back of the Hood closed.

Fold the Scarf Body in half and mark the center point with a removable stitch marker or safety pin.

Matching the center point of the scarf to the Hood seam, stitch the bottom edge of the Hood to the edge of the Scarf Body.

Weave in all ends.

Mattress Seam

Referring to Mattress Seam on page 44 and photos, thread a yarn or tapestry needle with matching yarn and close seams for mitts. ●

Kensington Pull-Through Scarf

Short-row shaping and a touch of lace provide the makings of a unique scarf with interesting construction.

· ·

Skill Level

 INTERMEDIATE

Finished Size
Approx 6 x 36 inches

Materials
- Stitch Nation Alpaca Love (worsted weight; 80% wool/20% alpaca; 131 yds/85g per skein): 3 skeins ruby #3920

  4 MEDIUM
- Red Knifty Knitter circle loom (31 pegs)
- Stitch marker
- Large-eye yarn needle
- Loom tool

Gauge
4 inches = 20 sts, 18 rows in garter st pat.

Exact gauge is not critical to this project.

Special Abbreviation
Slip stitch (sl): To slip a st, do not wrap the peg that is to be slipped, run the working yarn behind the peg.

Special Technique
Wrap and Turn: This technique is used to make short rows for shaping.

1. Work the number of sts directed in the pat.

2. At the end of the row, lift the next st off its peg and hold (Photo 1).

3. Take the working yarn to the front of the loom between the last peg in the row and the now-empty peg (Photo 2).

4. Bring the working yarn around the empty peg and in toward the center of the loom (Photo 3).

5. Place the loop back on the peg, so now there are 2 loops on that peg (Photo 4).

6. Work remainder of pat as desired.

Photo 1

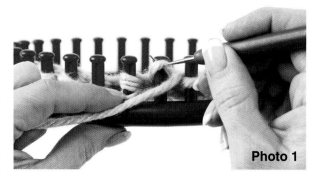
Photo 2

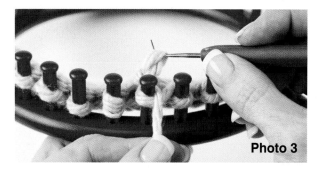
Photo 3

Photo 4

Row 2: Sl 1, k10, yo, k2tog, knit to end of row.

[Rep Rows 1 and 2 alternately] until scarf reaches approx 29 inches in length, ending with Row 2.

Increase rows

Row 1: Sl 1, p2, k5*, p1, k4, p2 (*this number will inc by 1 on each of the following rows).

Row 2: Sl 1, knit to the last 3 sts, yo, knit to end of row, moving each st out 1 to accommodate the inc of 1 st with the yo.

[Rep Rows 1 and 2 alternately] until there are 25 sts on the loom.

Center section

Row 1: Sl 1, p2, k15, p1, k4, p2.

Row 2: Sl 1, knit to the last 4 sts, yo, k2tog, knit to end of row.

Rows 3–6: [Rep Rows 1–2] 2 times.

Row 7: Rep Row 1.

End shaping

Row 1: Sl 1, k18, wrap next st and turn.

Row 2: K12, p1, k4, p2.

Row 3: Sl 1, k17, wrap next st and turn.

Row 4: K11, p1, k4, p2.

Row 5: Sl 1, k16, wrap next st and turn.

Continue in this manner, knitting 1 less st each row until only 2 sts rem, ending with an even-numbered row.

Next row: Sl 1, knit to end of row.

Next row: K3, *yo, k2tog, rep from * to last 2 sts, p2.

Starting with a knit row, work 8 rows in garter st (knit 1 row, purl 1 row).

Bind off using the flat-piece bind-off method (see page 8) and weave in ends.

2nd Half

E-wrap cast on 15 pegs. The last wrapped peg will be used as the first sl st in Row 1.

Row 1: Sl 1, p1, k4, p1, k5, p3.

Row 2: Sl 1, k2, yo, k2tog, knit to end of row.

[Rep Rows 1 and 2 alternately] until scarf reaches approx 29 inches in length, ending with Row 2.

Pattern Note

This scarf is worked in 2 symmetrical halves, and then seamed together in the center to form the scarf with an opening left at the far end to pull the flared end through.

Instructions

First Half

E-wrap cast on (see page 5) 15 pegs. The last wrapped peg will be used as the first sl st in Row 1.

Row 1: Sl 1, p2, k5, p1, k4, p2.

Increase rows

Row 1: Sl 1, p1, k4, p1, k5,* p3 (*this number will inc by 1 on each of the following rows).

Row 2: Sl 1, k3, yo, knit to end of row, moving each st out 1 to accommodate the inc of 1 st with the yo.

[Rep Rows 1 and 2 alternately] until there are 25 sts on the loom.

Center section

Row 1: Sl 1, p1, k4, p1, k15, p3.

Row 2: Sl 1, k2, yo, k2tog, knit to end of row.

Rows 3–8: [Rep Rows 1 and 2 alternately] 3 times.

End shaping

Row 1: Sl 1, k18, wrap the next st and turn.

Row 2: K12, p1, k4, p2.

Row 3: Sl 1, k17, wrap next st and turn.

Row 4: K11, p1, k4, p2.

Row 5: Sl 1, k16, wrap next st and turn.

Continue in this manner, knitting 1 less st each row until only 2 sts rem, ending with an even row.

Next row: Sl 1, knit to end of row.

Next row: K3, *yo, k2tog, rep from * to last 2 sts, p2.

Starting with a knit row, work 6 rows in garter st (knit 1 row, purl 1 row).

Bind off using the flat-piece bind-off method (see page 8).

Using yarn needle and long length of yarn, st 2 halves tog, starting at the end of the scarf. St to within approx 7 inches of the beg of the scarf. Fasten off. St 2 cast-on edges tog. Fasten off and weave in ends. ●

Camden Scarf

Simple drop-stitch elements paired up with just the right yarn is all you need to make an impressive statement.

Skill Level
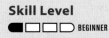 BEGINNER

Finished Size
Approx 4 x 70 inches

Materials
- Red Heart Curly Q (super bulky weight; 94% acrylic/5% polyester/ 1% spandex; 150 yds/85g per skein): 2 skeins totally teal #7958
- Green Knifty Knitter circle loom (36 pegs)
- Large-eye yarn needle
- Loom tool

6 SUPER BULKY

Gauge
4 inches = 12 sts, 12 rows in garter st pat.

Exact gauge is not critical to this project.

Instructions

Row 1: Purl cast on (see page 4) 12 pegs.

Row 2: Knit, slipping the first st.

Rows 3–8: [Rep Rows 1 and 2 alternately] 3 times.

Row 9: Purl.

Row 10: Wrap all 12 pegs in the row 5 times each, knit each st.

Row 11: Purl.

Row 12: Knit.

Row 13: Purl.

[Rep Rows 10–13 consecutively] until scarf is 49 inches long or to desired length, ending with row 10.

Work 9 rows in garter st, beg and ending with a purl row.

Bind off using the flat-piece bind-off method (see page 8). Weave in ends and block scarf if desired. ●

Soho Neck Warmer

For a fresh new look, these fun, spiraling I-cords will make a great impression.

Skill Level
◼☐☐☐ BEGINNER

Finished Size
Approx 5 x 24 inches

Materials
- Lion Brand Wool Ease Thick & Quick (super bulky weight; 86% acrylic/ 10% wool/4% rayon; 106 yds/ 170g per skein): 1 skein oatmeal #123
- Yellow Knifty Knitter circle loom (41 pegs)
- Large-eye yarn needle
- Loom tool
- N-13 (9mm) crochet hook
- 5 stitch holders
- 2 (1-inch) brown shank buttons

6 SUPER BULKY

Gauge
4 inches = 8 sts, 8 rows in St st.

Exact gauge is not critical to this project.

Special Technique
I-Cord

1. Cast on and wrap number of pegs as indicated in your pat.

2. Turn and wrap pegs as for knitting a flat piece and knit off.

3. Take the end of the working yarn behind the pegs from the peg on the right and over to the last peg on the left (Photo 1).

4. Wrap the pegs from left to right and knit off starting with the last loop wrapped. Pull down on your work to set the sts (Photo 2).

5. Continue in this manner until the I-cord is the desired length. Bind off following the flat-piece bind-off method (see page 8).

Photo 1

Photo 2

Instructions

Scarf Base
E-wrap cast on (see page 5) 12 pegs.

Row 1: Purl.

Row 2: Knit.

Row 3: Purl.

Rows 4–7: [Rep Rows 2 and 3 alternately] twice.

Divide for I-Cords

I-Cord 1

Using the first 3 sts in the row, work a 3-st I-cord until it is 20–22 inches long. Fasten off.

Move the sts from the first I-cord across the loom and out of the way.

I-Cords 2–4

Make a slip knot with the working yarn, and place it next to the next 2 sts on the scarf base.

Using the slip knot and the next 2 sts, create an I-cord that is the same length as the first.

On the last row, k2tog so that only 2 stitches rem. Fasten off. Move these 2 sts across the loom next to the previous I-cord made. Rep this method to create 2 more I-cords.

I-Cord 5

Using the rem 3 sts, create an I-cord the same length as the previous cords and fasten off.

Finishing

Place the ends of each I-cord on a separate st holder and remove from loom.

Loosely braid 4 of the I-cords, leaving 1 of the edge I-cords free of the rest.

Line up the I-cords and place the sts back on the loom with the 12 sts in a row.

Row 1: Purl.

Row 2: Knit.

Row 3: Purl.

Row 4 (buttonhole row): K3, k2tog, yo, k4, yo, k2tog, k3.

Rows 5–7: Rep Rows 1–3.

Bind off using the flat-piece bind-off method (see page 8) and weave in ends.

Sew 2 brown buttons to scarf base, opposite buttonholes. ●

Hyde Park Cowl

Add a touch of style and warmth by wearing this oversized cowl. It's the perfect way to cozy up this winter. The bigger-than-life stitches add extra style and interest to any wardrobe.

Skill Level

◼◻◻◻ BEGINNER

Finished Size
Approx 20 x 42 inches

Materials

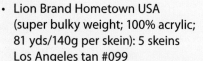

- Lion Brand Hometown USA (super bulky weight; 100% acrylic; 81 yds/140g per skein): 5 skeins Los Angeles tan #099
- Yellow Knifty Knitter circle loom (41 pegs)
- Stitch marker
- Large-eye yarn needle
- Loom tool
- N-13 (9mm) crochet hook

Gauge
4 inches = 8 sts, 8 rows in garter st pat.

Exact gauge is not critical to this project.

Special Technique
Making a Brim or Cuff

1. Knit as many rows as directed by your pat.

2. Reach inside and pull up the first row of cast-on sts. These will tend to be looser than the other sts.

3. Starting with the first peg, place the loops from the cast-on edge on each peg of the loom. Make sure that each peg has 2 loops.

4. Knit off pegs by pulling the bottom loop up and over the 1 you just placed on the peg.

5. Wrap and continue to knit as directed in the pat.

Note: After bringing the brim up, the first row will be very tight.

Pattern Notes
Hold 2 strands of yarn together as 1 throughout.

Due to the use of 2 pegs for each stitch, it is easier to use a crochet hook as a loom tool for this project.

To determine the desired length of the cowl, first measure around the upper body and arms of the wearer, then subtract 4 inches (as the knit will stretch) and use this as the measurement for the cowl.

Instructions
With 2 strands of yarn held tog and using 2 pegs as 1, e-wrap cast on (see page 5) 20 pegs.

Row 1: Purl.

Row 2: Knit.

[Rep Rows 1 and 2 alternately] until piece measures desired length, ending with a knit row.

From the center of the loom, pull up the sts from the cast-on edge and place on pegs as if making a brim for a hat.

Bind off with a purl st (see page 6), purling the st and the pulled-up loop tog before binding off each st. Weave in ends. ●

Westminster Eyelet Scarf

There isn't a whole lot you can do on two needles that can't be done on a loom. Get your first taste of lace by making this easy piece.

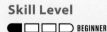

Skill Level
■□□□ BEGINNER

Finished Size
Approx 6 x 62 inches

Materials

- Patons Silk Bamboo (light weight; 70% viscose from bamboo/30% silk; 102 yds/65g per ball): 2 balls lotus #85425
- Green Knifty Knitter circle loom (36 pegs)
- Large-eye yarn needle
- Loom tool

Gauge
4 inches = 16 sts, 30 rows in lace st pat.

Exact gauge is not critical to this project.

Instructions
E-wrap cast on (see page 5) 25 pegs.

Row 1: Purl.

Row 2: Knit.

Rows 3–12: [Rep Rows 1 and 2 alternately] 5 times.

Row 13: K3, *(k2tog, yo), rep from * to the last 4 sts, k4.

Row 14: Purl.

[Rep Rows 13 and 14 alternately] until scarf is desired length, ending with Row 13.

[Rep Rows 1 and 2 alternately] 4 times.

Next row: Purl.

Bind off using the flat-piece bind-off method (see page 8) and weave in ends. Block scarf as desired. ●

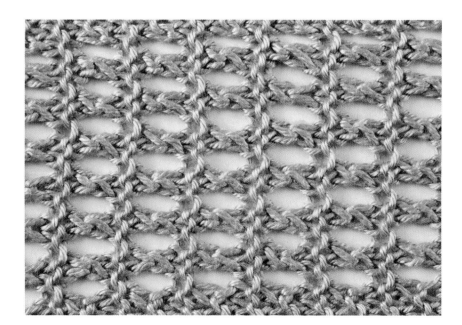

General Information

. . . .

Abbreviations & Symbols

[ ] work instructions within brackets as many times as directed

( ) work instructions within parentheses in the place directed

** repeat instructions following the asterisks as directed

* repeat instructions following the single asterisk as directed

" inch(es)

approx approximately
beg begin/begins/beginning
CC contrasting color
ch chain stitch
cm centimeter(s)
cn cable needle
dec decrease/decreases/decreasing
dpn(s) double-point needle(s)
g gram(s)
inc increase/increases/increasing

k knit
k2tog knit 2 stitches together
kwise knitwise
LH left hand
m meter(s)
M1 make one stitch
MC main color
mm millimeter(s)
oz ounce(s)
p purl
pat(s) pattern(s)
p2tog purl 2 stitches together
psso pass slipped stitch over
pwise purlwise
rem remain/remains/remaining
rep repeat(s)
rev St st reverse stockinette stitch
RH right hand
rnd(s) rounds
RS right side
skp slip, knit, pass slipped stitch over—1 stitch decreased

sk2p slip 1, knit 2 together, pass slipped stitch over the knit 2 together—2 stitches decreased
sl slip
sl 1kwise slip 1 knitwise
sl 1pwise slip 1 purlwise
sl st slip stitch(es)
ssk slip, slip, knit these 2 stitches together—a decrease
st(s) stitch(es)
St st stockinette stitch
tbl through back loop(s)
tog together
WS wrong side
wyib with yarn in back
wyif with yarn in front
yd(s) yard(s)
yfwd yarn forward
yo (yo's) yarn over(s)

Standard Yarn Weight System
Categories of yarn, gauge ranges and recommended needle sizes

Yarn Weight Symbol & Category Names	0 LACE	1 SUPER FINE	2 FINE	3 LIGHT	4 MEDIUM	5 BULKY	6 SUPER BULKY
Type of Yarns in Category	Fingering 10-Count Crochet Thread	Sock, Fingering, Baby	Sport, Baby	DK, Light Worsted	Worsted, Afghan, Aran	Chunky, Craft, Rug	Bulky, Roving
Knit Gauge Range* in Stockinette Stitch to 4 inches	33–40 sts**	27–32 sts	23–26 sts	21–24 sts	16–20 sts	12–15 sts	6–11 sts
Recommended Needle in Metric Size Range	1.5–2.25mm	2.25–3.25mm	3.25–3.75mm	3.75–4.5mm	4.5–5.5mm	5.5–8mm	8mm and larger
Recommended Needle U.S. Size Range	000 to 1	1 to 3	3 to 5	5 to 7	7 to 9	9 to 11	11 and larger

* GUIDELINES ONLY: The above reflect the most commonly used gauges and needle sizes for specific yarn categories.

** Lace weight yarns are usually knitted on larger needles and hooks to create lacy, openwork patterns. Accordingly, a gauge range is difficult to determine. Always follow the gauge stated in your pattern.

Skill Levels

BEGINNER

Beginner projects for first-time knitters using basic stitches. Minimal shaping.

EASY

Easy projects using basic stitches, repetitive stitch patterns, simple color changes and simple shaping and finishing.

INTERMEDIATE

Intermediate projects with a variety of stitches, mid-level shaping and finishing.

EXPERIENCED

Experienced projects using advanced techniques and stitches, detailed shaping and refined finishing.

Inches Into Millimeters & Centimeters

All measurements are rounded off slightly.

inches	mm	cm	inches	cm	inches	cm	inches	cm
⅛	3	0.3	5	12.5	21	53.5	38	96.5
¼	6	0.6	5½	14	22	56.0	39	99.0
⅜	10	1.0	6	15.0	23	58.5	40	101.5
½	13	1.3	7	18.0	24	61.0	41	104.0
⅝	15	1.5	8	20.5	25	63.5	42	106.5
¾	20	2.0	9	23.0	26	66.0	43	109.0
⅞	22	2.2	10	25.5	27	68.5	44	112.0
1	25	2.5	11	28.0	28	71.0	45	114.5
1¼	32	3.2	12	30.5	29	73.5	46	117.0
1½	38	3.8	13	33.0	30	76.0	47	119.5
1¾	45	4.5	14	35.5	31	79.0	48	122.0
2	50	5.0	15	38.0	32	81.5	49	124.5
2½	65	6.5	16	40.5	33	84.0	50	127.0
3	75	7.5	17	43.0	34	86.5		
3½	90	9.0	18	46.0	35	89.0		
4	100	10.0	19	48.5	36	91.5		
4½	115	11.5	20	51.0	37	94.0		

Special Techniques

Knitting With Beads

Threading beads onto yarn is the most common way to knit with beads.

Step 1: Before beginning to knit, thread the beads onto your ball of yarn using a bead threader. As you work, unwind a small quantity of yarn, each time sliding the beads towards the ball until needed. Pass the yarn through the loop of the threader and pick up beads with the working end of the needle.

Step 2: Slide the beads over the loop and onto the yarn.

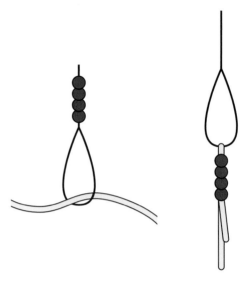

Mattress Seam

This type of seam may be used for vertical seams (like side seams). It is worked with the right sides of the pieces facing you, making it easier to match stitches for stripe patterns. It is worked between the first and second stitch at the edge of the piece and works best when the first stitch is a selvage stitch.

To work this seam, thread a tapestry needle with matching yarn. Insert the needle into one corner of work from back to front, just above the cast-on stitch, leaving a 3-inch tail. Take needle to edge of other piece and bring it from back to front at the corner of this piece.

Return to the first piece and insert the needle from the right to wrong side where the thread comes out of the piece. Slip the needle upward under two horizontal threads and bring the needle through to the right side.

Cross to the other side and repeat the same process, going down where you came out, under two threads and up.

Continue working back and forth on the two pieces in the same manner for about an inch, and then gently pull on the thread, pulling the two pieces together (Photo A).

Complete the seam and fasten off.

Use the beginning tail to even up the lower edge by working a figure 8 between the cast-on stitches at the corners. Insert the threaded needle from front to back under both threads of the corner cast-on stitch on the edge opposite the tail, then into the same stitch on the first edge. Pull gently until the "8" fills the gap (Photo B).

When a project is made with a textured yarn that will not pull easily through the pieces, it is recommended that a smooth yarn of the same color be used to work the seam.

Photo A

Photo B

About the Designer

Denise Layman has a bachelor's degree in Early Childhood Education and uses her degree to homeschool her four children—that is when she is not counting stitches and is done with her current row of knitting. She lives in Uniontown, Ohio, where she is also the president of the local knitting guild.

Denise has been designing patterns for knitting looms for seven years. She is also the author of *Learn to Knit on Circle Looms* published by American School of Needlework and is a featured crafter in *Craft Corps: Celebrating the Creative Community One Story at a Time*, by Vickie Howell. More of Denise's designs can also be found in the *Loom Knitting Pattern Book*, and on her blog: Knitting Without Needles, www.knitchat.com.

Photo Index

10

13

20

16

18

22

24

28

32

34

38

40

HOUSE of
WHITE
BIRCHES
PUBLISHERS
SINCE 1947

How to Knit Fashionable Scarves on Circle Looms is published by DRG, 306 East Parr Road, Berne, IN 46711. Printed in USA. Copyright © 2011 DRG. All rights reserved. This publication may not be reproduced in part or in whole without written permission from the publisher.

RETAIL STORES: If you would like to carry this pattern book or any other DRG publications, visit DRGwholesale.com.

Every effort has been made to ensure that the instructions in this pattern book are complete and accurate. We cannot, however, take responsibility for human error, typographical mistakes or variations in individual work. Please visit AnniesCustomerCare.com to check for pattern updates.

ISBN: 978-1-59217-318-1

1 2 3 4 5 6 7 8 9